ALL THE RAGE
IN THE AFTERLIFE
THIS SEASON

poems by

Marcus Cafagña

Finishing Line Press
Georgetown, Kentucky

ALL THE RAGE IN THE AFTERLIFE THIS SEASON

Copyright © 2023 by Marcus Cafagña
ISBN 979-8-88838-025-3 First Edition
All rights reserved under International and Pan-American Copyright Conventions. No part of this book may be reproduced in any manner whatsoever without written permission from the publisher, except in the case of brief quotations embodied in critical articles and reviews.

Publisher: Leah Huete de Maines
Editor: Christen Kincaid
Cover Art: Cole Closser
Author Photo: Jennifer Velasco-Cafagña
Cover Design: Cole Closser

Order online: www.finishinglinepress.com
also available on amazon.com

Author inquiries and mail orders:
Finishing Line Press
P. O. Box 1626
Georgetown, Kentucky 40324
U. S. A.

Table of Contents

I.

Second Chance 1
Monkey in a Brass Cage 2
Promissory Notes 3
Through a Glass, Darkly 4
The Starlite Drive-in 5
Friendly Fire 6
The Secret 8
Driving Cass Corridor Lost Near the Lodge 9
A Simple Plan 10
A Nameless Mother from Brooklyn 11
Her Side of the Story 12
La Pisca 13
Tattoos 14
The Hesperides 15

II.

The Law of Gravity 19
Far from the Eye of Heaven 21
Cornflake Christmas Wreaths 22
La Huelga, 1970 23
Honeymoon Hotel 24
Last Judgment 25
White Frosting 26
Reading Sex 27
The Death Sale 28
Nicely Woven Inside 29
Last Things 30
The Forgotten War 33
Recovery 36
Lost the Signal 37
After Hours at Paul Revere's Tavern 38
Revising History 39

III.

Last Meal 43
Rooming House 45
Forms of Life at Beggar's Banquet 46
By Dust 47
The Missing Toe 48
Mobile Home 49
Possessed 50
The Old House 51
Mowing 53
Wood Has a Memory 54
Asperger's Syndrome 55
The Shoplifting 56
For the Man about to Lose His Job at Dillons 57
Last Time 58
Morphine Sulfate 60
Louse 62
Diapers 63
Little Diego, the Muralist 64
Diego's Broom 65

Notes 66

Acknowledgments 67

Marcus Cafgña Biographical Statement 69

For Jenn

and

in the memory of Dianne

I.

Second Chance

Jenn tries not to make too much noise
when I'm home. She puts the dishes away
quietly. If a cupboard door slams
when I'm within earshot, she whistles
sweetly, so I'll know that no one
means me any harm. I promise to stop
obsessing over Dianne, only to give in
to thoughts of her and her suicide.

Jenn says she doesn't mind a husband grieving
his sad anniversaries, but she
shouldn't have to creep around the house
like a thief. She's fascinated, as I am,
by a woman who seemed so far
from the end of a rope, she'd pester
salesclerks in boutiques, dress
in thigh-high boots and tight skirts,
have half her face lifted by forty-four.

I marvel at Jenn's patience with my outbursts,
at the way I shrink into myself
when enraged, lose track of who I'm married to,
at the way she comforts me, her hand
on the back of my neck. She's trying
to give me whatever it is I need
to let my first wife go.

Monkey in a Brass Cage

Dianne felt a guilty dislike, a gift
from David, her first husband,
so she'd have someone to talk to
on nights he went drinking. From
the moment his drunken smile, handed
her the cage, she hated the black
eyes peering out, hated
to be alone with the constant
screeching, that
spidery restlessness, long greasy
fingers clutching hers
through bars, yellow
teeth bared at her bolting
the door against men fresh
from last call, hiding upstairs from their
drunken laughter, broken by the monkey's
frantic chattering. She knew
the monkey's face would lapse
into a sadness claimed by her husband after smashing
lamps and chairs, yelling himself
sober. In these moments, she vowed to love
the monkey, to cut up
apples and bananas. But mashing
her offerings, he flung them back.
One night, she came home to find the walls
and ceiling streaked with shit, his cage
vacant. She scribbled and taped
a letter signed *Kitty* to the fridge, lifted
the glad weight of a suitcase, savoring her
keys' brassy jangling as she lurched over ice.

Promissory Notes

She takes in the road her daddy
drove braking around the hairpin turn
where he finally lost control.
From her pickup's seat, she shudders
at what her headlights pass over,
the stretch of broken lines his blood once stained.
She can't forget the Cities Service station
he owned, the whiff of starch on the collar he wore
once bankruptcy reduced him to chasing rye
with malt and then his daughter.
Her thoughts pop and skip the ruts
of the country LP that played their prelude
to pulling off her training bra, sliding his belt
through the loops. Thinking of how sorry
he always was afterward, she has to laugh,
even at his vow to kill himself
and take her with him. Following
his final route, she's as lost in the wake
of any sudden silence as he was—
foot too heavy on the gas—before giving up
his grip on the wheel, passing out.
The sedan speeding him forward,
as the cigar box of promissory notes
flew from his lap like ticker tape
into the distilled air. The car ran
into the back of the carrier truck
she sees on the road ahead. In the dark
where he's gone, the eighteen-wheeler
stands stock-still as it did that night.
It looms on the shoulder as she slows
for a closer look at the long empty deck
which caved in her daddy's two-seater,
so that even his beheading
becomes the ghost of a promise he vowed
to keep, the one debt he paid in full.

Through a Glass, Darkly

Most nights, her father keeps the station
open late—downstairs in the service bay,
wrenches clank on concrete, grinding
casters send him rolling under cars. Behind
glass, on the second story, she can hear
engines idle and race, watch
the winged horse lighting
Mobilgas in neon's ad
nauseam. Color thrown against walls the blood
of her mother driven from here,
everything a reminder of absence—her volatility
matched only by his. Despite
the sideways drifting rain, she spies him
in uniform, standing beside the pumps,
downing beers, gauging how long
the storm should last. When it stops, his opera
will rise through her floor, the air outside so
still, his smoke rings turn to stone.

The Starlite Drive-in

The July after I turn thirteen,
my father drives me from my mother's house
down old dirt roads to the Starlite Drive-in.
Too old to play with children on the playground
between us and psychosis,
I watch their running shadows
invade the screen, superimposed on the movie.
We feel edgy already from the poorly synchronized
soundtrack crackling though the cast-iron speaker
gripping the driver's window, having never
seen a naked woman stabbed.
After *Psycho*, I can't
shower at either parent's house without
my pulse jumping. I don't
tell my father how even the cries
of those kids playing gave me the creeps,
boys' shadows swinging eerily back and forth
across the screen, weightless, attached to nothing.

Friendly Fire

1

I can't recall which cousin swore Aldo's knees had locked
in a nervous shake from the combat he'd seen. His knees would
pump, all ways, as he shifted the weight in his chair,
rocking himself as if he was back to being the age of nine.
His hands trembled as he appeared to move toward
somewhere safer in his head. I never dared to ask
why his face was cast in permanent five o'clock shadow
like a man who needed a shave. I wondered if it was true
that a hand grenade burn he suffered from an exploded
pineapple, olive-drab, dropped accidentally by a comrade
clearing the beaches of landmines before a botched
invasion of the Italian coast in October of 1943,
had instead blown up in poor Aldo's face.

2

Raised with the terror of Blackshirts breaking in
to arrest and deport his father for helping Jewish friends
escape Italy, Aldo lived, after this,
in Michigan. There, he wrote aspirin commercials
for Bayer and a war novel no one would ever read.
When it came his time to fight, his infantry division had landed,
only to be pinned by gunfire, in Naples—his place of birth.
How he must have felt to stand—a Yankee GI
on the volcanic soil of ash deposits after the fall
of Il Duce. He had then to live his life in the afterglow
of surviving a frag grenade blast, close range.
He had then to avoid his mother and sisters at times,
preferring to stay hidden in a cloud of Lucky Strikes.

3

I never knew what to say at family gatherings
as I sat, at dinner, across the table from him—
when his knees would start to knock, when he couldn't
seem to sit still. He was ever on high alert,
expecting radio-guided bombs to burst
any minute over grayed skies of Detroit.
Always, he smiled the bull-faced smile
of the defeated, preparing himself
for the worst—for some detonation of gunpowder
to release into our air, knocking just him out.
He would be revealed to us then the young soldier
he was when the southern region of his face
had been set on fire—doused hot silver, afterbirth.

The Secret

The shop looked closed from the street,
candlelit, crystal balls and shiny tapestries
framing the costume
the fortune teller wore, her magician's
cap pulled down over her wig. We watched
her shuffle and cut the Tarot deck,
then spread the cards
face up, across the felt. Dianne gasped
at the picture of a man hanging
upside down from a tree, cleared her throat
as the fortune teller told us a Four
of Cups crossed with a Two of Cups meant
the lovers depicted would separate. Dianne's nails
dug into the back of my hand. *Are you
saying my husband and I are going
to separate?* The fortune teller's eyes
burrowed into the cards before
looking up. *They might
mean that.* Candlelight
trembled under Dianne's breath as she
rose and snatched her twenties off
the fortune teller's table. *What are you,
some kind of fraud?* The woman's
eyes widened and followed
us out the door. In the car,
Dianne said, *the bitch thinks we're headed
for divorce. I'll never divorce you.*
That week she climbed to the top of the built-in
basement bookshelf, tied one
end of electric cord around a beam and noosed
the other around her neck, before she half
jumped, half fell, to her death. I still
see the fortune teller in her silly
cap, the look of shock then
recognition in her eyes that saw
how far Dianne would go.

Driving Cass Corridor Lost Near the Lodge

when the rear tire blows
and I bundle out

wind lashing my hair like a flag

toward linoleum shacks chain
link hubcaps and old doors
that whisper of your old man's
garage the summer
the draft took you from us

*how strange these streets looked
after Saigon the shadow of grenade burns
a beard I can't shave*

dark as men thawing still
in fire rising from barrels and blue
curl of hand-rolled smokes I squish

wingtips through mud unable
to stare into this ring of faces without
seeing yours years
younger under a toque

*the smile I lost on airplane glue
on potholes that jarred me loose
through vacant lots*

and lives abandoned like cars
with handles roped together
tight as a huddle of men
passing Night Train back

and forth though heat brims close
enough to singe eyebrows *I can't
find you anywhere*

A Simple Plan

Weeks before she took her life,
she asked me to picture

an afternoon in autumn,
the hour softening toward evening

when a husband and wife have
time to veil their kitchen walls

with plastic sheets, and stretch
transparent wings over windows

and doors to keep any air
from escaping. With a cat

in each lap, we could
bid the world adieu. If only

I'd switch on the gas without
lighting the jets and let us

die together, at last, like a family.

A Nameless Mother from Brooklyn

Riding the el train to the end of the line
is how your son learned to leave home.

Some nights after work, you ride those
same empty cars over the neighborhood

beyond Avenue K, not knowing how
or where to miss him. What's the use

of recalling simple gestures—curly knots
of his hair you once untangled, sweat

mopped off his ears—how far must wainscoting
lift its border from the wall before it cracks?

Lives lived out in tiny kitchens, some
desperate enough to jump from heights like this,

prayer books open to *Blessed be His name…*
You chop brains and cold cuts

at the deli until your hands feel hard-boiled,
eyes rubbed raw as onions, when all this talk

on the radio of junkies dying in the street
seizes your chest like a rusty percolator—

that's when the cupboard you open groans
on empty, when your favorite dress hangs

in the closet like a worn-out apron.
The night rails sing you a litany,

the names of all the lost fathers and sons,
the names of all the lost fathers and sons.

Her Side of the Story

After my husband rose and dressed, the wind
wove a gauze of heat over Avenue
of the Americas, and not a cloud obscured the blue breath

that hung overhead. Not one helicopter
burning hamlets of the Mekong. What song was it
we used to sing

for the island we lost, if not the Taino
Caribbean bamba of a door gunner
over the South China Sea, the faith he held in my dark

brown eyes, listing off the ports?
Below the groove of ankle bone the osteopath
found the tender hurt,

my Hector's pain like so much surf, receding.
Shipped home to her examining table, he sobbed
as she massaged the tendons of the gunshot foot,

the part of Vietnam that got so bad
he self-inflicted. I watched her sooth the bullet hole,
the nerves that spark the spine

and the retrenched wound of memory give him
release. Now he's back on these
El Barrio blocks, where lightning bolts, not carbines, snap

and the thrumming through walls is Radio Azul,
the salsa beat he remembers as his last
civilian dance.

La Pisca

It means picking the crop,
cleaning what lettuce heads remain
after the bruised and moldy are tossed.
Tuvimos una diferente visión de los E.E.U.U.
We imagined a different U.S.

Working in shifts beside me were mothers,
fathers and their children from Tijuana, Juárez,
working from dark to dark.
No nos tengan pena. Nosotros mismos no nos compadezemos.
Do not pity us. We do not pity ourselves.

College boy, I learned to bend and kneel,
to twist and snap the roots, to hoe
the stubborn plants up and chop them free.
Sin trabajo, no hay vida.
Without work, there's no life.

One summer only, I picked a field where coyotes
talk families into crossing the border,
into shacks without bathrooms or water.
Vivimos cómo lagartijas, cómo las ardillas, cómo las ratas.
We live like lizards, like squirrels, like rats.

Juanita's crippled hand, Juan, with a knife in his shoe.
I tried shifting my weight from one knee
to the other, but the ache wouldn't stop.
En Mexico, és asi cómo un hombre se hace hombre.
In Mexico, that's how a man becomes a man.

I can't forget the stoop of a life not mine, every head
paid for by mothers' arthritic backs and fathers'
chopped-off fingers, by children choking on pesticide.
Y ahora nos mandan de vuelta.
And now you send us back.

Tattoos

Inked at dawn
off the highway in a shack, the horizon
backwashed and colorless.
Mermaids dangled from anchors
in midsummer heat while eight balls
collided into oblivion
and pythons peeled from walls.

We cut our sleeves
to show them off, drove
home through pockmarked streets over
shrubless lawns, dancing Marlboro
eyes out cracked Chevy windows.
Nothing beneath us save
the metal around the windshield
holding broken glass in place.

We knew what we believed.
I wish I were sure now
that the sharp black lines of devils
and bobcats grown indistinct
over muscle have lost
their menace as I catch
low beams in the rearview and turn
into the road ahead.

The Hesperides

Nobody loves to see a hitchhiker
in sawed-off denim shirt,
with a skull-and-crossbones tattooed sleeve.
While noon glints off windshields
of slowly passing cars, and sunblinds
their interiors, I hallucinate
sedans tight with women, milkweed down
rides visible waves of wind. Visions
of California hook my thumb beyond
Ohio, beyond the turnpike
solitude unless
some trucker's cab door opens.

II.

The Law of Gravity

> *Parking spaces luxuriate like civic*
> *sandpiles in the heart of Boston.*
> —Robert Lowell

Strolling down the gallery
of cells, a bemused guard

hands me hot coffee,
but with the sugar spilled

along the seam of the cup
my fingers feel the burn.

And there's no one to thank
for the seven hundred miles

I hitchhiked from Ann Arbor
only to be caught trespassing

in an underground carpark
in Boston, for the free trip

to jail. A conga line
of cockroaches stretches

down to my commode
from the tier of cells

on the floor above,
where I can hear a door

roll shut and someone
in the drunk tank, crying.

Under my wall-mounted bunk,
I uncover a pair of old pants,

shoes, eyeglasses—
signs I might be lucky,

that the man here before me
has died or walked out naked.

Far from the Eye of Heaven

The skin divers found him in a car
at the bottom of a lake. Such a quiet kid,
mole-faced, skinny, salty-haired, cousin Saul
who walked nights alone on an L.A. beach.

A teenager without girlfriend, gang,
or job. His mother drew cartoon characters
for Hallmark and never understood
his restless need for motion, like his father's,

for the road. But we all missed Saul
those last few weeks, guessing
dope or suicide. None of us says
anything now he's so long dead.
Maybe it's best he left no lover, no note,
best not to know if this is what he wanted.

Cornflake Christmas Wreaths

Dianne's aunt bakes cookies we hang
from the bough of the needled tree. We pay
Fran a visit, stuck
on the sofa with lecherous Uncle Chuck,
whose thick skin white elephant pale
distrusts anyone with a swarthy hide, winks
and smirks jokes he hopes will
upset us—like the one
about a dumb wop who asked
the hooker to pay *him*—throwing
back his head to laugh alone. Even
if Fran knows of her husband's attempts to get
my wife, his niece, into bed, she couldn't
manage without him—but slides
sideways in her wheelchair like she's sick
of his voice. Paralyzed on the right
side of her body, she squeezes
the bad hand with the good, as if
awaiting a miraculous
return of feeling. She likes to fuss
over Dianne's rings and bracelets, who doesn't
care how the cornflake and marshmallow
concoctions taste
that Fran makes with her good hand
before she hangs cookies from the boughs
of a needled tree.

La Huelga, 1970

The year Chavez calls for a lettuce boycott
we pose beside a shopping cart as husband and wife.
Still kids in school, we fake honeymoon smiles
to give Safeway checkers the sense
we're customers. The Salinas U.F.W.
has put us through our paces
picking heads until our weary muscles tell us
why any farmworker, paid piecemeal,
would wave the red flag in protest.

The produce manager is quick to repeat
that growers had denied Mexican children
were dying from pesticide their crop-dusters sprayed.
Led through back rooms and coolers,
we double-check the lids on crates
of iceberg unloaded by Teamsters.
We plan to kiss-and-tell on a union
so rotten they stamped their label,
instead of ours, all over some sweetheart deal.

Honeymoon Hotel

Instead of tearing off our clothes in the shimmer
of the Hotel Diana's satin sheets, we check out.

Roman streets that fall are scorching hot, full
of pickpockets and, to our surprise,
public masturbators. Once renowned

for pinching American women, Italian men
thrust out their hips. On the bus,
behind Dianne, a young Lothario unzips

and stains her black crepe de chine
skirt. Instead of marble
walls and fresh cut narcissus,

the pensioni Porta Maggiore rooms
come with a fan that blows
flakes of rust in our eyes. The iron

edges of twin beds pushed together dig
into our flesh no matter what
position we try. Instead

of a Roman tub, the tin can shower backs up,
a flood she must wade through.

If there are sights, we can't see them without
cursing the country my grandfather
came from. Trevi Fountain's romantic shimmering

makes us daydream of the satin sheets
in which we could've tumbled
into daybreak.

Last Judgment

Wandering through Vatican City
a mother and son in peasants'
rags tip their soot
streaked faces up. Empty palms
out, they take us in. I dig
for the money belt inside
my pants, contorting my body for a few
thousand lire. Pickpockets know
easy marks, especially turisti.
Up close, the grime makes me sick
to my stomach, ashamed
to be a tourist. The Sistine Chapel undergoing
restoration's dust of centuries
lifted, the painting's clean
half unnaturally bright doesn't match
what I've seen in books. Scaffolding rises
into the barrel-vaulted ceiling, our view
of Genesis obscured. No hand
of God extends as we file
past the *Last Judgment* to our idling
bus. On the Chapel stairs, nearly
unrecognizable, in Roman
sandals and frock, a carton of smokes tucked
under her arm, the boy beside her sporting
a fish-themed Hawaiian shirt. Their scrubbed
features sunlit, hair still
damp from bathing, neither
will acknowledge us, struck
dumb to find them in their best
finery, decked out as Michelangelo
never would have painted them.

White Frosting

Ate wedding cake
at midnight, danced
out the screen door
wearing only a t-shirt, and didn't

mind the windows dark
in other apartments, her

skin cantaloupe ripe
on our balcony,

a sweetness and abandon
she threw to the ants.

Reading *Sex*

This picture for us: our favorite
model secretly dark-haired and stern,

daughter of a groom who leads the Rossetti crew
on a terrible dance. We obey

two laws: one horizontal and the other strung
implacably straight, as if the plumb

line of gravity were physical
conscience, the ocean inside

each of us made visible
as ice cracking in a cocktail, as in our worlds

set suddenly at right angles, or our Italian girl
playing the part to perfection with props,

this cup of air, this prow and stern, this
alabaster snap of the whip.

The Death Sale

Shock deadens to sorrow,
deadens to leaves crackling; our daughter holds
a yard sale with little
stickers on anything
of Dianne's: a hundred
belts, counting the plastic one she
practiced with, enough
blush to paint a thousand masks, a table
full of vitamins, another strewn
with books by her idol, Tennessee Williams,
his restlessness, his sleeplessness, like hers,
their streetcar named Desire going nowhere.
It's my idea to sell the furniture, washer, dryer,
waveless waterbed, as if now
that she's gone, I'll never
need to wash or sleep again. My neighbors
don't mind robbing the grave. One
teenage girl opens a compact, thinks
she looks beautiful in too much make-up,
smears on the garish rouge from Dianne's
French maid get-up. Everything sells except
her stiletto heel menagerie. Skeletal
thin, a woman like you
know who in white scrubs models the French
platforms, sighing *Oh,*
Paris, loves her legs in Milanese knee-high
boots while cradling a pair
of pumpkin-colored pumps. In Filipino
English, she says no barrio
nurse back home could afford them. It hurts
to know they are just her size—that
they mean to her what they meant. I won't
take her money, say if Dianne
were here, she'd want her to have these shoes
she hoped would help her walk out
of one life and into the fantasy of another.

Nicely Woven Inside

A snapshot of my late wife holding up
a necktie for the camera,

it's the tie's back she displays—its inner
lining. *Nicely woven inside*

the vendor blurted. I took
the photo on a Roman street shortly after

she noticed the unstitched triangular
flaps of fabric, when the tie's casing

came undone. Her manicured fingernails
pinched the silken folds open

to reveal what I'd missed—a hand
painted nude. I caught her

before she burst into the kind of laughter
that came first in snorts, then tears.

And though the joke was on me, I had to laugh
at what the vendor, in his poor English,

must have really said: *naked woman inside*.
I can't be sure, but I think he winked.

Last Things

She's alone inside the red ceramic urn
on the mantel of our living room. A lifelong blonde,
dressed in red—all the rage in the afterlife this season.
She's ash and bone, waiting to be stirred by the wind

off the mantel of our living room. A lifelong blonde,
she's dressed to walk out the door of a smoke-filled duplex
in her ash and bone, just waiting to be stirred by the wind
before her mother, done for the day with beauty,

walks in the door of the smoke-filled duplex.
Still her mother's daughter, thrilled with getting caught
by the floorwalker, she's done for the day with beauty,
done with any thought of French tips or glitter.

Still her mother's daughter, she's thrilled to get caught
shoplifting by the floorwalker with gold hoop earrings,
with French tips with a splash of glitter,
in pumps that echo between the racks of silk.

Shoplifters, the floorwalker with gold earrings joked,
will be hung up like camisoles, like seamed stockings,
joked as her pumps echoed between the racks of silk,
her hair pinched in spit curls. Every night, dead,

hung up like the camisoles and seamed stockings
she stuffs into the bodice of her jumper,
her hair pinched in spit curls. Not the floorwalker
but her, dead as the drunken father she's been waiting for.

If she could stuff into the bodice of her jumper
all the things in her life that never happened:
the drunken father who left her waiting at the window,
or having forsaken her dissertation to attend Hairesy.

All the things in this life that never happened:
all the pennies never tossed into Trevi Fountain,

having forsaken her dissertation to attend Hairesy,
the beauty school where she learned to bleach wigs.

Always the lucky penny destined for Trevi Fountain.
Stranger to the Styrofoam head of the practice dummy
at the beauty school where she hated bleaching wigs
until her fingers burned with peroxide

from the Styrofoam head of the practice dummy's
false hair, that she combed until it wilted,
until her fingers burned with peroxide,
like flower petals, and she breathed in the fumes,

and the false hair she combed through that wilted.
And now, the stitches that vanished like a trail
of flower petals, and her breath like fumes.
Gone is her white blouse, her black skirt.

Gone the stitches of that vanished trail
the plastic surgeon left behind her ears.
Gone her white blouse, her black skirt,
her jeweled belt. Gone the scent

the plastic surgeon left behind her ears,
that like my whisper held her close,
close as her jeweled belt. Gone the scent
of her flesh, her body when I found her.

Gone the whisper that would have held her close
that Sunday morning, in that madhouse basement
where I found her neck in a noose. A body
stiffening to dust, swirling a silver eddy

where she'd been. This Sunday morning, up there
on the mantel, she's alone without her diamonds
and rings. Now, her dust swirls a silver eddy
where she's been, her golden bracelets—sealed in.

Now, she's alone without her diamonds or her rings.
Like a sacrament, these things she couldn't bear
to part with. Her bracelets, too, sealed
inside a sandwich baggie the undertaker handed me

like a sacrament. These things she couldn't part with
—all the rage in the afterlife this season—
in a sandwich baggie the undertaker handed me
now that she's alone inside the urn.

The Forgotten War

1

These are the glasses of Charles Bye,
the frames I bought him to try.
He always meant to pay me back.

This is his birth certificate,
and the words I read at his funeral.

Here are the stars and stripes
bearing a seven-gun salute.
After firing the guns, they fold
the shell casings into the flag.

2

He had a few changes of clothes
in a bus station locker, a razor,
a toothbrush, enough for a week's stay.

Panhandler, working the building
where I worked, he asked for my help.

The bus station was closing as we loaded
his belongings into my car.

3

He was tired
        of staying up
                all night

in Chinatown's
           movie theaters
                   or restaurants

where he could buy
> a bowl of noodles
>> and sit in a corner.

4

The room we found for him
    had no running water
and shared a bath down the hall
    with five other rooms.

5

Perhaps I helped Chuck because he reminded me
of my father, the same careful mustache.
Not exactly like my father, but once
I took him into my life, that was it.

Here's his passport picture.
He wanted safe passage
from the dangers of the street.

Chuck was clean, meticulous.
He outlined his room with roach powder,
made me take off my shoes and wear sandals.

Rainy days,
he stayed in, bathed, and read
until someone
else wanted the tub.

6

He cut out
articles proving
the secret

operations
on unconscious
soldiers,
again
and again
told me
he was the
subject of
a conspiracy
in Korea.

The Army
put a chip
in his
stomach.

7

Chuck told me he read
that even monkeys
deprived of physical contact
become asocial.

Our one awkward Christmas,
when I hugged him,
he seemed surprised.

8

The V.A. admitted him, but never
admitted he was sick
from anything but liver failure, his skin
yellowed, his stomach swollen. After
he died, the doctor, staring
at his clipboard, muttered he
didn't know why.

Recovery

When the phone rings she answers
to hear she has cancer.
Where an hour ago we sat, mother
and son, at the window,

watching fallen leaves rustling away,
now a word moves her lips
in a mantra, as if to diminish
her body's betrayal. And in its wake,

uterus gone, she hears some upside-down
surgeon saying *hysterectomy, more
radiation*, some insomniac nurse with
a tray of pills, chanting *swallow, swallow.*

Lost the Signal

Like someone first learning to speak,
his words come out halting and few.
Not so long ago, he could outtalk us all,
before the chemo left my father's memory
stuck. I think he still knows who I am,
because he tells me to go home,
though my plane just landed. But I'm not sure
I know him since the cancer fenced
him to a hospice bed—his body
so shrunken, his shock of hair
turned silver, the veins in his arms
bulged blue against his crepe paper skin.
As I blather on about nothing,
he shifts his gaze from the TV to eye me
through a pair of tortoise shell rims,
touches a bony index finger
to his temple and says, *Lost the signal*.
I shrug, not knowing what the hell
he means. Not taking his eyes off mine,
he points his finger again, this time
at his forehead, and repeats the words,
Lost the signal, like someone losing
his mind. He rolls those dark eyes
toward the window, where my stepmother
has hung a blue stained-glass bird,
its ruby wings spread in perpetual flight.
Instead of us speaking, he wants
to share this moment of his dying, this
silence between father and son, where words
hold no meaning. Later, here in the kitchen,
when I tell Beth how he touched
his head and told me he lost the signal,
she says, without emotion or pause,
*Yeah, that's what he says if the batteries
in his hearing aid are running low.*

After Hours at Paul Revere's Tavern

After the bar closes, it's sobering to catch
a glimpse of my distorted
reflection in the beer sign's
blinking mirror. These nights
weigh more than bar stools
I stack on tables, or cases of empties clinking
against my hip, the old Hoover I flick on,
its steady hum failing to soothe. Swizzle
sticks, butts, bottle caps, snap
through. I have to hurry. Nothing will ever
be clean enough: both
restrooms hot and cramped,
the walls in the Women's sweating
to the linoleum. Below a partition, I bump
what could be somebody's arm.
Flinging back the stall door, it's only
Rita, the bartender, passed out, beside
the bowl, a fifth of Four
Roses tipped on its side, a strand of pumpkin
hair swaying on her breath, mouth gone
slack and mournful, until
a look of clarity prints itself on a forehead
crosshatched with tile. I, half-lugging her
back to the bar, minister her with cold
coffee, but she wants to sleep it off, so I flop
her rubbery body across three stools.
No matter how I plead or shake
she curls into a fetal ball and, snoring, slips
off the makeshift bed as she helped me
once when I was falling. I stock
the cooler, wipe counters, and ready
the bar for the morning crowd—and vacuum
around her.

Revising History

Driving the Escort, she confessed—over the radio's
Motown throb—to lunch with an old lover.

Jealous, I flung my door open
and threw myself from the moving car—

centrifugal force dumped me
into the fast lane, alive, but foolishly alone.

Cars dodged me as I trampled the median's
ornamental grasses. I shouted so she, idling alongside,

could hear and, sticking her head out the window,
shout back. The hell with the angry drivers

leaning on their horns and changing lanes behind her!
The hell with what they thought of our soap opera!

A week later, the ambulance I called screamed
to our townhouse. If only I hadn't left her

to find sweet rolls. The paramedic, who followed me
back down to the basement, mentioned the blue

necklace the ligature left on Dianne's neck
but not the face that looked surprised. After

the wake, I paced the basement floor, convinced
if I closed my eyes, she'd magically reappear.

If I stood on the spot her feet never touched,
her Hebraic aura might wrap me in its wings.

I wish I'd forgiven her that day we fought,
after she parked and opened the passenger door

and begged. Her lunch with Jack, and calls
to friends were farewells: if only I had known—

III.

Last Meal

In spite of doctor's orders, she eats
meat and greasy
potatoes after weeks of nothing
but miso and rice for a bleeding colon, cheeking
her meds, refusing to go to therapy, curled
most nights at oblivion's edge. Sometimes
she lurches from bed terrified until
I flick on the light and open the closet
door wide enough to see no jewel
thief inside, her one black boot
overflowing with diamonds
and gold where she'd left it. I want to remember
that Burger King booth, to think
of her hunger as the opposite
of depression, to forget her stories
of the little girl her father called Cotton
singing and twirling on top of a bar table
for his drunken pals, try not to smell
the undercooked meat she was raised on,
the fatback cured in salt. Even strung-out,
manic, Dianne dresses up, paints her lips
a deep red, the way she would for Daddy.
She puts gravity to the test, tells me
she tried to hang herself with a belt
too flimsy for the job. I don't believe her
even after she's given our cats away,
convinced the white one is a witch,
even after the bad cut and dye job sears
her cotton-candy blonde to orange. So long
as her caustic wit burns,
she'll be okay. The more she chews
and swallows, the better she begins
to look. The next day,
coming home with the *Times*
I find her, hanging by the neck. Screaming,
I cut her down, try to break her fall
with outstretched arms. My last moments

with my wife spent alternating *Come back,*
with mouth-to-mouth, so help me,
there's a second when her eyes
open and recognize me
with all my faults looking back,
her lips unclench, as though
startled awake: she seems on the verge
of speech; she seems as if
she has a choice.

Rooming House

It's the headlights exposing the smudged window,
bass rumbling through floorboards,
the crack of spark plugs like gunshots.

It's rats and two bathrooms for sixteen people,
plaster flaking from the ceiling like dirty snow.
It's the couple next door screwing in the heat.

On the fire escape's rusty steps
the kid with the ponytail drinks
and tokes while the neighborhood

decays after he's stripped
his walls of paneling to reveal a hole like a jaw
gaping, holes

scaring the front walk, hole his fucked-in-the-head father
shot in the wall—what a world
of plaster couldn't mend.

Forms of Life at Beggar's Banquet

Cockroaches do not like rock and roll,
not the gutbucket blues the Stones cover band
blares in drunken revelry from a bar stage
five floors below in the basement of this
building in East Lansing. Cockroaches do not love
loud electric guitars or rumbling bass.
They like neither feedback nor distortion.
How they disdain the hiss of white noise,
four-four time. How they propel their hairy
back legs in any direction away from music.
Up through crack and crevice, they vibrate,
four-four time. Oh cockroaches, they like
to touch, with their sticky antennae, stucco walls—
walls of these two-room flats where it costs
too much to live above a bar named after
the Stones comeback album, the needle of all
we once thought hip. Not until the stage
empties and the six-legged intrusion again
descends the subterranean circles of hell,
will the pulse of our suffering be unplugged.
Not until the sun at last lights the sky above
a bar in East Lansing named after the greatest
rock and roll party, not until our lives end,
can we all come back as roaches.

By Dust

I dug headfirst into lint traps
that were mine to empty, each
steam-driven cubbyhole swirling with particle
dust, cutting class to crawl
through the campus Laundromat. In

a kind of coffin, I lay on my back
without shame, beneath king
size dryers thinning my breath

to a wheeze. Dorm rats shot me
passing glances, since it's rude
to stare at a man's gray skin
masked by bandanna and dust. No
stranger to their disco lifestyle, I craned
my neck inside one trap after another in case a few
coins, like a cheap tip, had trickled
from designer pockets. I never
begrudged them their ivy halls,
so long as I didn't end up someone's servant
like my old lita after she landed here.
In an age of flappers, she waited

on bluebloods, who passed through her
ladies' room. She sheltered me.

Were she still alive, I think my Anna Corona
would forgive her dropout grandson
now that I'm el professor, my sleeves
smudged with chalk, and the rasp
in my voice the only
reminder of that dust.

The Missing Toe

For M. J.

Since the surgery, he walks these halls
with a cane, colleagues nipping at his heels.
Since he's diabetic, he can't skip a meal
without the risk of getting the insulin shakes.
Or a trembling in his hands that starts
in the middle of class one morning.
Hard to shock this younger generation
with his blood sugar running low.
And yet the spectacle of their professor
lost in space, as if rendered speechless
by the independent and dependent clauses
of the sentence he'd diagrammed on the board,
made everyone in class pay attention.
Couldn't say how long he'd forgotten
where he was—surrounded by pupils—
the lack of sugar sapping his muscles
and his mind, too far gone to tell
that from *which* or *who* from *whom*.
Said he should be thankful for the bad foot,
though. He has a good job, a good wife
and three dogs to comfort him at night.
All that's missing from his life is a little toe.

Mobile Home

Blue shag and mini drapes
in shadow boxes, laminated
cornice board that fifty years

have split, its metal
skirting torn off for the wrecker
to haul away. No one
listens to this radio or bothers
to shut the window against
the wind that rattles a magazine's unread
pages. Headlights, her only

companion, swept
between narrow walls. My aunt
we all thought was rich
spread doilies and dusted
her way through this world,
until lumps swelled

against her throat and chemo
dropped hair into her lap
and she left
us thrusting our hands
under beds, reaching behind tufted
white headboards for baby
food jars stuffed
with dollars we never found.

Possessed

If Dianne were alive, she'd pin me
to a chair, straddle a leg
on either side of mine.

After all this time, she'd still
search my face. Even when
we were dating, she considered it

a duty to rush the ferocity
of her love with no warning
but the rustle of her skirt.

The Old House

Not the old neighborhood,
the streets choked with shotgun shacks,
or the dilapidated ranch we used to rent. Can't

say I miss the landlord we never met
or the opossum that snored under our car. Don't
care if I ever again see the man next door,

his German shepherd on a chain, or the deer
decoy he shot arrows at when Bambi
was out of season. Mornings

after dropping off our little boy at school,
I still drive by the old house to spy
on what chump braves that leaky
exoskeleton now, betting whoever he is
is sick to death of breathing
hard air. Jenn and I joke

that on the day we moved out, our cat
hid behind the fridge
rather than give up eating cave crickets.
Who could forget how hot that house got
when the A.C. conked? To get air
flowing I had to walk up rickety steps
around the side of the house,

to a utility closet riddled
with spiders and their mummified hoard
to duck at the fuse box.

Our first place together, and we didn't
care about housekeeping, dust
polishing every surface, the living room strung
with Christmas lights we couldn't bear
to disconnect. Every night a party—even

that winter when the rusted-out
chamber of the octopus furnace cracked,
and the Santa-shaped plumber dropped his wrench
with a whistle, and swore it was the oldest
almost working furnace he'd ever seen.

Mowing

The figure of Adrian cursing the mower
reminds me of lawns I cut at his age—shirtless,
sweating, sunburned—jailhouse
tattoo a strand of barbwire cinching his neck.
Over and over the engine fails, spews
smoke and the bitter
sweet smell of gas. I know what it is to hate
the hand that hired me with a loathing
bigger than a starter handle, the engine
that won't turn no matter how I pull.
Even when it does, the blade's dull
from so much grass, and thistle too tough
to shorten. Just like that, I could've abandoned
somebody's yard half-mown. My two-stroke
contraption looked a lot like his: muddy and caked
with oil. Embarrassed by my luck,
from this air-conditioned chair, I know
how bugs and mice invade once grass
around a house goes wild. Even
with rust flaking off his car—his wife
pregnant with twins—I'll have to fire him,
but not today.

Wood Has a Memory

This house has a crack in it,
and that crack has baby cracks,
and every crack in the family
runs up the walls in every room.
The door to the bedroom doesn't
close as it should, and the door
to the bathroom doesn't close at all.
The floorboards in the living room
are sinking. In my son's room, too.
The man tells me the foundation
needs to be shimmed after lifting
the house back on its blocks,
because wood has a memory.
Wet boards warp when they dry.
Wood never forgets a drought
or a record rain nor forgives
the earth this side of the river,
expanding only to contract,
shifty with limestone and clay.

Asperger's Syndrome

This time there's a rhythm to it,
the boy flapping his hands on things,
the fireplace mantel and each end table.
There's a joy in running his fingertips
along the wainscoting, over the backrest
of every chair on his route
through the living room. His breath
comes faster and faster as he circles
the square dining room table—
round and round. His bottom lip
sticks out, as if he is under a spell,
walking, in his red and gray
Angry Birds pajamas, to the beat
of a song on Sesame Street. His father changes
the channel. The boy keeps chasing himself—
this kid on the march, with his dark hair
flung to one side, pounding his feet
around the table, until the room
begins to shake—seven, eight laps
before he stands still and plays
a video game of Batman and Robin,
makes his wand pop gunfire.
Missiles and bombs explode here
on the screen, but it's a bottle broken
blocks away that rattles in his head.
His father no longer asks him to stop
spinning around in circles in the kitchen,
a boy balanced on the ball
of only one foot, his arms extended.
Turn after turn, in whirling pirouettes,
the walls seem to spin. The sensory fix
leaves him breathless, dizzy
enough, at last in space, detached.

The Shoplifting

The butcher, in his blood-stained apron, catches me red-handed.
To the crime of stuffing
a ten-cent bag of potato chips into the unzipped belly of my jacket,
I plead guilty.
The snack-size Lay's falls out. With his meaty forearms, the butcher
drags me, in my sneakers,
by the collar, over a greasy floor back behind the deli counter.
It's 1968,
and yet I'm held prisoner in the last corner market
of an era gone by.
Sitting on an overturned milk crate behind the deli case, I can't
feel the breeze of a rotating fan
turning back and away before reaching my face. Chopping up
cuts of meat with his cleaver,
the butcher tells me I'm lucky I'm so young. He's not calling
the cops. I fight back
tears of relief. The number I give him to call is not my mother's.
Sick with the stench
of rotting pine and newsprint, I want to remember feeling free.
Then, bells chime
over the front door, and I see my father in his tie-dyed t-shirt.
To spite a forehead
creased with worry lines, his dark hair is cut in Beatle bangs.
It comes as no surprise
he was busted for pot in 1948, that he wore the mug shot
of a smuggler's shame
in *The Detroit News*, that his pop whipped him with a belt.
To hear my father humor
the butcher is to know shoplifting is just kid's stuff.
If my father's fixed gaze holds mine,
it's not for the stealing, it's for keeping my cool. Shouldering
his mod medieval pouch,
he leads me back outside to a bucket seat in his Triumph TR4.

For the Man about to Lose His Job at Dillons

The barista turns up his brogue
as I wait at the counter for him
to pour my Americano with room.
Clouds of steam push up
around his rusty mutton chops,
coating his worry lines in sweat.
He's getting laid off
after Christmas, after he's done
tearing down the roaster,
the grinder, the espresso machine.
He's been working in the Ozarks
for a company in Kansas
owned by Kroger's in Ohio.
Because only this one market
turns a profit, every store
in the chain is closing.
The one that was across the street
is now a career center,
where folks like my friend
will file for unemployment.
Friend. That's what he calls
me today after he snaps
on the lid and I tip him and turn
to go, but I don't
even know his name.

Last Time

I could as well have chosen to leave my wife
for such a drunken night at the Battlefield Inn.
But I'm not that guy, only friends with that guy
who calls me for a ride when he can't drive
without blowing sober on the breathalyzer
hooked to his steering wheel. I'm the friend
with nothing better to do than to strap
my five-year-old son in the car seat
at high noon and taxi a man who's lit
to the gills across town, park, and wait
beside a blue empty swimming pool
while he's fast-talking the guy at the desk
into letting him a room he won't trash
this time. I tell myself it's not my lot
to sit in my car with my son in a hot motel
parking space, my legs glued to the upholstery.
But who am I kidding? While I nod my head
to the radio, several hungover middle-aged men
are on a balcony above, awakened to the sun.
I watch them lean against the shaky iron railing,
wince in the blowback of the day's first butt.
The one wearing a Royals cap doesn't whistle,
but hoots. This makes the others crane their necks
for a better view. Afraid for a second, I think
Royals Cap is hooting at me and my boy.
But in the rearview, I see it's not us
in the car they're all gawking at but instead,
my friend, who's emerged in his handlebar mustache,
under a neon sign. He throws back
his curly hair, shows his face in half a laugh.
The party is not going to last as long
as he thinks, but today he's the guest of honor,
making his triumphant return. I can hear
his accent as he totters, gone three sheets
to the wind. My friend, who dares to float
free of the family life to which I cling,
lives like he could die one night

soon in his sleep. He stands worn,
like the brown canvas bag thrown
over his shoulder, his big hand waving
for us to back up the car—to go.
Pushing out his lower lip, my son asks,
Are we just going to leave him here?

Morphine Sulfate

1

There's one that makes the head nurse whistle—
those x-rays of his backbone.

When his back really hurts,
like it did after eighteen-hour shifts in the E.R.

How many pain patches does it take
to pry pleasure from pain?

Two scoped knees
and one total shoulder later.

2

A pocketful of quick-release tabs
is his backup for the jones he means to shake,

his stop-gap, his joint in the ashtray to fire up
next time the sun burns fluorescent

against the heavens, or just in case clouds
held close by rain have to part.

This is him, hanging on,
ten milligrams a day.

3

This is him, speaking all about recovery
to the newbies at the detox center.

Alert with hurt instead of nodding in a haze
of 200 mgs. More pure than any junk out on the street.

He can press the flesh with short-timers, show
how a man with a spine so twisted

only a radiologist could love, stays out
of a wheelchair. Off the stuff he cannot smoke.

Louse

You gave ancient Egypt the itch
and pub-crawled the Roman Empire.
Now you bring shame on me as a father.

No tree oil, no thin-toothed strip
of plastic will rid us of the wingless.
Not since you scaled the sweatband

of some classmate's Cardinals cap
to my son's scalp, not since my wife
had enough of me, and I moved out.

Parasite, you infect me, too,
with fangs drenched in gore—my son's
and mine—our blood-sealed pact.

You make me homesick in my rental.
My son? You make him worry
about the louse I turned out to be.

You are a tiny particle that flits
between us, a radiant energy
along our spectrum of absence.

Dear lord of little beings—
though I poison the nit of your loins—
I know I must give thanks.

Diapers

My son wants nothing more to do with them.
At four-and-a-half, he's made
his declaration of diaper independence.

He's four. But my son isn't old enough
to understand age. When he's twenty,
I'll be seventy. When he's forty, I'll be gone.

Even now, standing before the chalkboard
in a room full of twentysomethings,
I need leak-lock protection. My doctor says

this is what happens to men at my age—
we just blow up. After the war,
the first disposable was fashioned

from a shower curtain by a single woman
sweating over a Singer, who thought
snap fasteners safer than safety pins,

who thought of it as a boat holding water.
And what of the prostate, swelling as it ages?
The gods, what were they thinking?

Where is the elegance when both the father
and the son begin and end their lives—
bare bottoms swaddled in diapers?

Little Diego, the Muralist

We don't know what to make
of his scribbling on the walls
of our living room, on the walls
of our kitchen, his bedroom,
in red crayon. Diego will draw
on any available surface,
ignore our pleas not to,
ignore the easel we bought him.
We're so far past the point
of trying, my wife and I wonder
if these random lines and circles
are his protest against
a grown-up world that says No!
to the same artistic impulse
as Rivera's. Just yesterday,
on the front door, he drew
what appears to be a series
of storm clouds. With one red
cloud each, he's adorned
the nine white panels of the door.
But this time, Jenn and I
admire what he's drawn,
as if, in molten wax, our little boy
has blessed the scorched air
of Mexico with clouds
that might soon deliver
the blessing of rain and miracle
of the desert blooming green.
He smiles with a knowing look
when we say the old door
never looked so beautiful—
festooned as it is with red clouds
and the promise they hold.

Diego's Broom

When I take the child-sized broom off its hook
and hand it to him, my little boy says, *Broom
clean? Broom clean?*

I answer, *Yes, but be careful.*
Though what harm could a two-year-old
do to a store aisle stacked
with go-karts and beach balls?

Diego pushes it faster and faster
over the floor, as the blue
strands collect dust. I watch until

I must abandon
our shopping cart and hurry after him.

When I say, *Never, never, run away from Daddy,*
fearing what he can't understand, Diego
smiles up at me with his brand-new tooth.

Notes

Some of the English quotations used in "La Pisca" can be found in *Shadowed Lives: Undocumented Immigrants in American Society.* Edited by Leo R. Chavez (Harcourt Brace, 1992). The Spanish I translated with Gloria Vando.

"Far from the eye of heaven" is a quotation from the Charles Baudelaire poem "The Irremediable" in *Les Fleurs du Mal.* Translated by Richard Howard (David R. Godine, 1982).

"Reading *Sex*" is a cento.

The epigraph for "The Law of Gravity" is a quotation from the Robert Lowell poem "For the Union Dead" in *Life Studies* and *For the Union Dead* (Noonday, 1956).

"The Forgotten War" is inspired by a Thomas G. Carroll oral history.

"Mobile Home" is dedicated to Ted Kooser.

"Recovery" is for Alan Shapiro.

"Morphine Sulfate" is for Tom Lowry.

"Louse" is after Yusef Komunyakaa.

Acknowledgements

Grateful acknowledgement is made to the editors of the following publications in which these poems first appeared (some in slightly different versions or under different titles):

Arts & Letters: "Friendly Fire"; "Lost the Signal"
The Bellingham Review: "White Frosting"
The Bridge: "Driving Cass Corridor Lost Near the Lodge"
Cave Region Review: "Asperger's Syndrome"; "The Forgotten War"; "The Old House"; "The Secret"; "Wood Has a Memory"
Cedar Hill Review: "The Hesperides"
Chiron Review: "Morphine Sulfate"
Connotation Press: An Online Artifact: "Honeymoon Hotel"
Crab Orchard Review: "After Hours at Paul Revere's Tavern"; "La Huelga, 1970"; "Last Judgment"; "Through a Glass, Darkly"
Devil's Millhopper: "Monkey in a Brass Cage"; "A Nameless Mother from Brooklyn"
Elder Mountain: A Journal of Ozarks Studies: "Diapers"; "Diego's Broom"; "For the Man about to Lose His Job at Dillons"; "Revising History"; "Second Chance"
Gingko Tree Review: "Little Diego, the Muralist"; "The Starlite Drive-in"
Harvard Review: "Reading Sex"
In the Black, In the Red: Poems of Profit and Loss: "La Pisca"
Long Shot: "Rooming House"
Many Mountains Moving: "By Dust"; "La Pisca"
Midwestern Gothic: "Cornflake Christmas Wreaths"
Moon City Review: "The Death Sale"; *"Nicely Woven Inside"*; "Possessed"
Paddle Shots: "Last Time"; "The Law of Gravity"; "Mobile Home"
Passages North: "Tattoos"
Quarterly West: "Last Things"
Rattle: "Last Meal"
Slant: "The Shoplifting"
Slipstream: "The Law of Gravity"
Southern Poetry Review: "Mowing"
The Southern Review: "Far from the Eye of Heaven"; "Promissory Notes"; "Recovery"; "A Simple Plan"
The Teacher's Voice: "The Missing Toe"

Some of these poems also appeared in the following anthologies or exhibits:

Beyond Hills: Contemporary Ozarks Poetry; East Lansing Poetry Attack; Nature Adores a Vacuum; Pittsburgh Post-Gazette; Readings @ The Tap Room; River Rat Review; Verse Daily; Yonder Mountain: An Ozarks Anthology.

Mil gracias to Leah Huete de Maines, Kerry James Evans, April Ossmann, Jim Daniels, Betsy Sholl, Jeffrey Ethan Lee, Cole Closser, David Moolten, Anthony Isaac Bradley, Jill Breckenridge, Michael Burns, Jenny Crews. A special thanks to Roger Weingarten.

Marcus Cafagña is the author of three books of poetry, *The Broken World*, a National Poetry Series selection, *Roman Fever*, and *All the Rage in the Afterlife This Season*. His poems have also appeared in T*he American Poetry Review, Arts & Letters, Harvard Review, Quarterly West, Rattle, The Southern Review,* and *The Threepenmy Review,* among other journals and anthologies. Born in Ann Arbor, Michigan to a family of immigrants, many of his relatives fled fascism in Europe to settle in Detroit or New York. He teaches poetry writing at Missouri State University. He moved to the Ozarks from Philadelphia, where he coordinated the Painted Bride Art Center Poetry Series, and from Pittsburgh, where he served as a visiting writer at Carnegie Mellon University. Praise for his previous books: Pulitzer Prize-winning poet Yusef Komunyakaa in his foreword to *The Broken World* describes Cafagña's poetry as "This tabulation of broken things (beings) tells us what we must know and confront in order to make ourselves whole in the modern world." Joyce Peseroff writes in *Ploughshares*, "Cafagña doesn't muddle the past with false nostalgia or the future with false hope, but…interprets the signals of silenced lives and provides a measure of redemption." Keith Taylor writes in the *Ann Arbor Observer*, "Much like Sylvia Plath's *Ariel,* Cafagña's poetry is written in extremity. But there is one big difference. Whereas Plath wrote to save herself, Cafagña writes out of compassion for those he loves, and the knowledge he gains is perhaps a more painful one."